CONTENTS

THE FORMATION OF THE AUSTRALIAN IMPERIAL FORCE - 1914

The steps that led to the outbreak of the war are well-known. Once Germany had violated Belgium's neutrality, Great Britain was compelled to respect its duty to protect the small country and thus entered the war on 4 August. The gathering storm had been apparent for some time and Australia had already made provisions for home defence. However, the day before Great Britain declared war on Germany, Australia had offered her navy and 20,000 troops to serve under British command wherever required. This offer was promptly accepted and the Inspector-General of the Australian Military Forces, Brigadier-General W.T. Bridges* was immediately tasked with raising troops. This was undertaken by using volunteers that were part-time militia members, as well as a small number of regulars. The Australian Imperial Force (AIF) officially came into being on 15 August 1914. The British Government initially proposed two brigades of infantry, one of light horse, and one of field artillery, but Bridges suggested the formation of a single infantry division and one light horse brigade. Bridges stated that : "Each unit will represent a State and distinct locality, officers and men thus bringing with them the cohesion, comradeship, and local association which are such valuable elements in promoting the highest standards of discipline in the field and of gallantry before the enemy."

As was the case in the mother country, the Call to Arms was a huge success and by September there were sufficient numbers to form another infantry brigade and a further two light horse brigades. As the war dragged on and the casualty lists lengthened, the number of volunteers dwindled. There were two referenda held under the leadership of Australian Prime Minister, Billy Hughes to decide on the implementation of conscription. The first referendum was held in October 1916 and was narrowly defeated. A second, in June 1917, was more clear-cut and the attempt was massively defeated. The AIF remained, therefore, a volunteer force. By the end of the war, there were five infantry divisions and two mounted divisions, as well as other units.

*Brigadier-General (later promoted to Major-General) Sir William Bridges was shot by a Turkish sniper on 15 May 1915, subsequently dying of his wounds three days later. He as succeeded by British Lieutenant-General William Birdwood.

✦ Australian recruitment posters.

✦ Men enlisting in Perth, 1914. "It was a feeling that England was the mother country. We were only a colony anyway, and although we'd been given independence, we were so tied to Great Britain that when she was in trouble it was just automatic, a feeling of 'this is your duty' .....It was automatic. Every man from the first day off was a volunteer... some of them, they'd walked for two, three days... it was a remarkable expression of loyalty. I doubt if it would ever happen again." Charles Bingham, AIF.

✦ HMAT Orvieto was a troop transport with the Albany convoy.

THE DEPARTURE FOR WAR - 1914

1 November 1914 saw the departure of the first contingent of the AIF from the port of Albany in Western Australia. Thirty-six troop transports, escorted by cruisers, carried 20,000 men and women of the AIF and 8,500 of the New Zealand Expeditionary Force. The men initially believed that they were setting off for England but news that winter conditions there could not guarantee decent billeting conditions, meant that the decision was taken to send the AIF to the warmer climes of Egypt. This would also mean that their first adversaries would not be the Germans.

The convoy reached the Suez Canal on 1 December and began disembarking two days later in Alexandria. The AIF then settled down and began training.

THE DARDANELLES CAMPAIGN - 1915

The Dardanelles campaign was the brainchild of Winston Churchill, the First Lord of the Admiralty. There was stalemate on the Western Front and the objective was to capture the strait, then capture Constantinople (Istanbul); thus knocking the Ottoman Empire out of the war and opening up a sea route to the Russian Empire.

The Campaign involved British and French forces and began with a naval bombardment of the coastal defences in March 1915. The troop landings began on 25 April 1915. The AIF landed at Anzac Cove and gained a tenuous foothold on the steep and rocky terrain. The Turks proved to be tenacious fighters and every yard was hard-fought. As the allied forces desperately tried to push inland so the Turks showed equal desperation in forcing them back. The campaign ended in stalemate and, ultimately failure. Field Marshal Lord Kitchener arrived at Gallipoli on 13 November and surveyed the situation for himself. He subsequently recommended evacuation. For the remaining 20,000 men of the AIF this was carried out in secret from 18-20 December 1915. AIF losses at Gallipoli were 26,111, of which 8,141 lost their lives. The Anzac legend was born. The survivors returned to Egypt. Their next destination would be the Western Front.

✦ 1st Battalion men in a trench near Lone Pine, Gallipoli.

✦ A German trench club used in trench raids.

✦ Australians in the trenches at Bois Grenier, 3 June 1916.

✦ The sector held by the 1st Anzac Corps up to mid-July 1916.

ARRIVING IN FRANCE - 1916

The 1st and 2nd Divisions arrived in Marseilles, France in March 1916. The 2nd Anzac Corps, with the 4th and 5th AIF divisions remained in Egypt to continue their training.

The units were transported by train to the St.Omer – Aire – Hazebrouck region in northern France and were slowly introduced to the conditions they would face on the Western Front.

Their first experience of trench life was in the Fleurbaix sector, a then quiet part of the frontline that was known as the Nursery due to the fact that the British Expeditionary Force placed newly arrived units there in order to acclimatise to life in the trenches. Between May and mid-July, the 1st Anzac Corps (1st and 2nd Div. plus the New Zealand Division), held ten miles of frontline from the river Lys north of Armentières to the German-held village of Fromelles.

FIRST CONTACT WITH THE GERMANS

Trench raids were carried out by both sides, both in order to gain moral ascendancy and to gain information concerning the units opposite. A large-scale German trench raid was launched on 5 May 1916 against men of the 20th Battalion holding the Bridoux Salient near Bois Grenier. Many casualties were caused by the preparatory bombardment and eleven Australian prisoners were taken back to the German lines. Another major blow in this engagement was the capture of two Stokes mortars, new weapons that the British were keen to keep secret. The officers in charge of these weapons were subsequently court martialled.

Another German raid was launched on 30 May in the Cordonerrie Salient; losses for the 11th Battalion numbered 131 with 47 killed and 11 taken prisoner. These raids left the Australians in no doubt that they faced a skilled and resourceful enemy. However, the Australians soon learned to hit back equally as hard. A week later, six officers and sixty men, all volunteers from the 26th and 28th Battalions, launched their own raid against German positions near Armentières. They captured three prisoners and killed seven of the enemy. These raids were important in helping the AIF gain confidence.

✦ The Mills Bomb was especially effective in trench warfare.

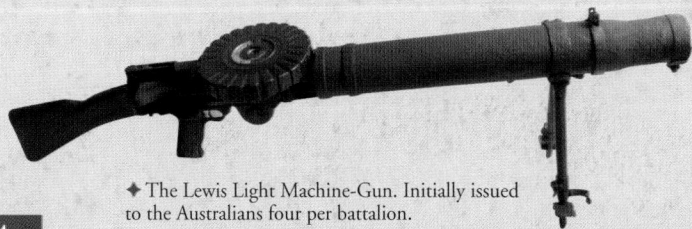
✦ The Lewis Light Machine-Gun. Initially issued to the Australians four per battalion.

✦ Arriving on the Western Front meant that new and better-suited equipment was issued. Men were issued with the new War Office Pattern Shrapnel Helmet.

FROMELLES

The Franco-British offensive on the Somme began on 24 June with a week-long artillery bombardment. The men went over the top on 1 July, with the British attacking north of the river and the main French effort to the south. That sunlit Saturday has entered British folklore as the worst in its military history. Losses were staggering, over 19,000 British men lost their lives that day and close to a further 40,000 were wounded. Piece-meal attacks continued into the first half of July and the Australians soon found themselves called upon for this titanic clash of arms. The 1st, 2nd and 4th Divisions (1st Anzac) were notified that they were to move south towards the Somme. The 5th Division, which had only recently arrived was to remain in the nursery sector. However, they would also be the first to go into action.

The objective of the attack was to take the high ground at Fromelles and Aubers Ridge, an area where this had already been tried, and failed, in 1915. It was also hoped to draw German reserves away from the Somme. The 5th Division of the AIF was to go into battle alongside another inexperienced division, the British 61st. The low lying ground opposite Fromelles was boggy and crossed by ditches and a stream. The attack was launched on the evening of 19 July. What ensued was nothing short of disaster. The deadly and machine-gun ridden Sugarloaf Salient was not captured and the British and Australians were hit by enfilade fire. The fighting continued into the night and the German counter-attacks forced the Australians back from any ground that they had gained. Losses for the 5th Division were appalling with 5,513 casualties. The Division was badly mauled and would not be ready for further action for quite some time. The British 61st Division had sent into the attack roughly half the Australian number and had suffered 1,547 casualties. The German 6th Bavarian Reserve-Division losses are estimated at between 1,500 and 2,000.

Australian confidence in British command was badly shaken by the failed attack at Fromelles.

PHEASANT WOOD

Australian researchers were convinced of the existence of burial grounds near Fromelles. A subsequent survey confirmed the existence of burial grounds at Pheasant Wood. Exhumations were carried out and 250 bodies were recovered, 173 of which were Australian. DNA research on the Australian men allowed for the identification of 75 men. The first of the Pheasant Wood men were buried in a new cemetery in 2010.

PLACES OF INTEREST

The Museum of the Battle of Fromelles, located next to the Pheasant Wood Cemetery, opened in 2014. Visiting details can be found at www.musee-bataille-fromelles.fr

Also nearby is the Fromelles Australian Memorial Park with its remains of concrete bunkers and the moving Cobbers sculpture by Peter Corlett. A few hundred yards away is V.C. Corner Australian Cemetery and Memorial.

✦ The Cobbers sculpture (by Peter Corlett) at the Australian Memorial Park. It is a representation of Sgt. Simon Fraser of the 57th Bn. He wrote a letter in the days following the battle and it was quoted in Charles Bean's official history. "I could not lift him on my back; but I managed to get him into an old trench and told him to lie quiet while I got a stretcher. Then another man ... sang out 'Don't forget me cobber'. I went in and got four volunteers with stretchers and we got both men in safely."

PERSONAL EQUIPMENT

British-made 1908 Pattern equipment was used by Australian troops.

✦ Australian infantryman with 1908 Pattern equipment.

✦ The magazine held ten rounds of .303 ammunition.

✦ Australian leather infantry equipment. Great Britain was unable to fully supply Anzac units at the beginning of the war, indeed, the cotton webbing manufacturers were working at full production and even then, not capable of supplying the burgeoning new armies. The Australians therefore made a set of leather equipment that was similar in design to the British 1908 Pattern equipment. The leather equipment was not very popular and the cotton webbing equipment replaced it as soon as was possible.

✦ SMLE rifle made in the Australian Lithgow arsenal.

THE SOMME — POZIÈRES

"Pozières ridge is more densely sown with Australian sacrifice than any other place on earth." Charles Bean, Australian official historian.

The German-held bastion of Pozières lay upon a high plateau that afforded good observation. The British launched several attacks, both from the direction of Ovillers and Contalmaison. These attacks stalled however and General Haig passed on the responsibility for the capture of Pozières to Lt. Gen. Gough's Reserve Army, of which the 1st Anzac Corps was a part.

The attack began on 22-23 July with the 1st Australian Division advancing from the south-east and the British 48th Division from the direction of the Albert- Bapaume road. The ruined village was captured and the Germans withdrew to their O.G. defence lines to the north and east of the village. The German high command ordered the recapture of Pozières and began to pour concentrated artillery fire into the rubble. It was said that the Australians experienced the heaviest artillery barrage of the entire war here. When the 1st Australian Div. was relieved on 27 July, it had suffered over 5,000 casualties. The nightmare was not over for the Australians ; the 2nd Australian Div. was next in the line and in two days lost 3,500 men. A fresh attack on the O.G. lines was made on 4 August and succeeded in their capture. The Australians now controlled the ridge and could see unspoilt countryside towards Courcelette and Bapaume. The 2nd Div. was relieved by the 4th Australian Div. on 5/6 August and in its twelve days in the line, had suffered 6,848 casualties. The Germans made one last attempt to recapture the vital high ground but were repulsed by the Australians in a fierce hand-to-hand fight. By the end of the battle, Pozières was nothing but a crater field strewn with the dead of both sides.

✦ The same view seen in August 1916.

✦ Captain Ivor Stephen Margetts, 12th Battalion. He was killed at Pozières on 24 July. His grave was subsequently lost and he is commemorated at the Villers Bretonneux Memorial.

✦ The main Albert – Bapaume road running through the German-held village of Pozières in 1915.

ALBERT JACKA VC

At the eastern end of the village is the highest point of the Somme battlefields. Today the position can be seen from many areas thanks to a high telecommunications aerial. Opposite stands a small piece of land where the Australian and French flags fly side-by-side. This was the site of the windmill, a building that had stood there before the war and which had been fortified by the Germans. The loss of this high ground was a blow to the Germans and they were determined to win it back. The subsequent barrage of 6 – 7 August has been described as the heaviest ever experienced by Australian troops. During a lull in the shelling, the 14th Bn. made its way up Centre Way, a shell pummelled trench choked with dead and wounded men. The 14th Bn. was relieving the survivors of the 25th, 26th and 28th Battalions. Albert Jacka VC, placed his platoon near the Elbow in OG2. The German barrage caused terrible casualties to the men of the 14th and many of Jacka's men had been wounded. Due to the heavy shell fire, Jacka sheltered in an old German dugout with his men. At 4.45am the barrage lifted and the Germans attacked in strength. A German rolled a grenade down the steps of the dugout, wounding and stunning some of the men. Jacka shot the German with his revolver and mounting the stairs, saw that the German attack had passed by him and was now a few hundred yards forward. Approaching him was a large group of 48th Bn. men that had been taken prisoner. Jacka and seven men from the dugout charged into the Germans, half of whom threw down their weapons and the other half returning fire. The Australian prisoners took up the abandoned German rifles and joined in the fight. Other units rallied and the German attack was thwarted. Jacka had been wounded seven times but his brave and inspired leadership saved the day. Charles Bean, the official historian, stated that Jacka's counter-attack "stands as one of the most dramatic and effective act of individual audacity in the history of the AIF." He was awarded the Military Cross but many felt that he had earned a second VC.

WHAT TO SEE

Just before the village is the Pozières Military Cemetery with 2,756 graves and the Memorial to the missing of the 4th and 5th Armies of 1918 with 14,644 names. Upon entering the village there is a memorial to the King's Royal Rifle

✦ Albert Jacka VC, MC and bar. He was the first Australian to win the Victoria Cross (Gallipoli).

Corps, a little further along is the lane that became known as Dead Man's Road. The 1st Australian Div. Memorial is next to the former German Gibraltar strongpoint. Passing through the village, the Australian Memorial stands on the site of the windmill where the O.G. lines passed on Hill 160. Opposite is the Tank Corps Memorial, it was from here that two tanks first went into action on 15 September 1916. There are walking trails available for downloading from the Australians on the Western Front 1914-1918 website. The Tommy café is a must for visitors to the area with a fascinating private museum displaying locally found artefacts from the fighting.

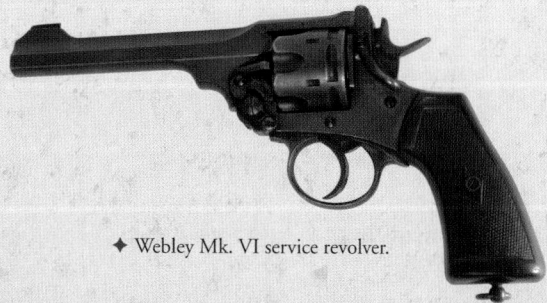

✦ Webley Mk. VI service revolver.

MOUQUET FARM

The road from Pozières to Thiepval takes the visitor past the site of what was perhaps the most fought over ground during the Somme battles. Mouquet Farm, known as Moo-Cow Farm to the Australians, sits on a ridge overlooking the valley in front of Thiepval. The farm today is sited to the right of the original emplacement.

The farm became a regimental headquarters to the various regiments of the German 26. Reserve-Division and was used as a signalling station for German artillery during the failed British attack on Thiepval. As the fighting progressed and nearby Pozières fell to the Australians, Mouquet Farm protected vital high ground that prevented any progression, via the rear, towards the Thiepval strongpoint that had held off all attacks since 1 July.

The 16th Battalion of the 4th Australian Division was the first to go into action at Mouquet Farm on 10 August, they made gains but were subjected to an artillery barrage of unprecedented ferocity. The 2nd Australian Div. came into the line here on 22 August, followed by the 4th Australian Div. on 3 September who captured the farm, but discovered that the Germans had built an inter-linking defensive network below ground. A German counter-attack pushed them back again. The Australians were relieved in the Mouquet Farm – Pozières sector by the Canadian Corps on 5 September. Total Australian casualties around Pozières and Mouquet Farm were in excess of 23,000.

✦ An Australian officer's service revolver still in its holster, found near Mouquet Farm in 2011.

"The flayed land, shell-hole bordering shell-hole, corpses of young men lying against the trench walls or in shell-holes; some – except for the dust settling on them – seeming to sleep; others torn in half; others rotting, swollen and discoloured." Charles Bean, Australian official historian.

✦ Mouquet Farm sector, June 1916.

✦ The same area in September 1916.

THE SOMME WINTER

Following the terrible losses suffered in six weeks on the Somme (23,000 casualties with 6,750 dead), the AIF was sent north to the Ypres sector where new drafts of reinforcements were used to rebuild the shattered battalions. The AIF returned to the Somme at the end of October. It was also at this time that the first referendum was held back home over the issue of conscription. The Prime Minister, Billy Hughes, knew that the losses suffered on the Western Front would be difficult to replace with the current volunteer system. He was, however, narrowly defeated and forced to form a coalition government.

The men of the AIF took over the sector near Flers, an area that had been fought over in late September and where tanks had gone into action for the first time. The churned up battlefield made movement incredibly difficult and the onset of winter brought untold misery to both sides.

✦ A muddy trench near Gueudecourt, December 1916. "We live in a world of Somme mud. We sleep in it, work in it, fight in it, wade in it and many of us die in it. We see it, feel it, eat it and curse it, but we can't escape it, not even by dying." Edward Lynch, Somme Mud.

As the Somme campaign petered out, the AIF fought at Gueudecourt in an attempt to push the line forward from the low-lying and waterlogged valley and up the ridge beyond where the town of Bapaume could be seen a few kilometres distant. It was in the aptly named meteorological trenches (they were given weather-related names, such as Stormy Trench) that the AIF settled down for what would be one of the worst winters on record. With their supply lines stretching back to Longueval it could take men up to six hours to cover just over two miles. An Australian military chaplain said that, "The German was no longer the great enemy, it was the winter." The men suffered from the cold and wet conditions; there were many cases of frost-bite, trench foot and trench fever brought on by lice infestation.

The Soldiers' Manual of
FOOT CARE & FOOT WEAR
by Capt Cecil Webb-Johnson
6d. NET.
INDISPENSABLE TO OFFICERS AND MEN
DRYDEN PUBLISHING COMPANY LTD

✦ The men who suffered from trench foot and frost-bite "left the trenches on the long journey to the rear. Their feet wrapped in cotton–wool, they limped along or negotiated a particularly difficult piece of ground on the shoulders of a passing digger." William Devine, 48th Battalion Chaplain.

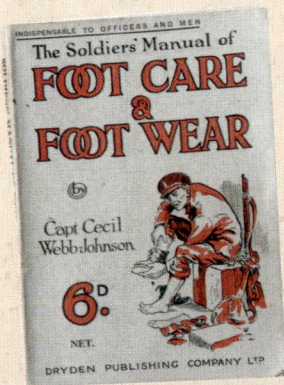

Boots The Chemists
SPECIAL PREPARATION AGAINST
✦ A battlefield found tin of anti-lice powder.

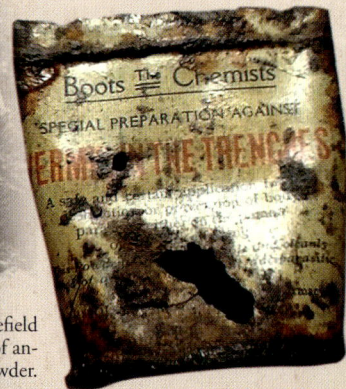

MAINTAINING MORALE — HELP FROM HOME

The Australian Comforts Fund was created in August 1916 from various organisations at home that had been created in order to provide the men with items that would be useful on active service. Fund raisers were held in Australia and women kept themselves busy knitting socks, scarves and balaclava helmets. Money raised was also used to purchase goods that were sold to the men via small canteens near the front-line. Men were also provided with hot drinks and food, as well as reading material. The work of the ACF was vital in maintaining morale.

✦ A make-shift Australian Comforts Fund canteen near Longueval, Somme.

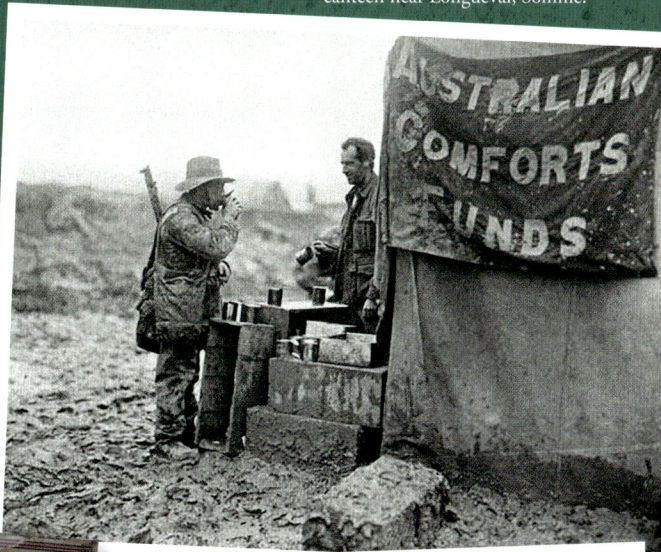

KNITTERS GET BUSY!

WAR CHEST WANTS SOCKS

Appeal for 150,000 Pair

K is for Knitters
   (We each must be one);
N is for Needles,
   Whose work has begun;
I is for Interest,
   (Which makes us take part);
T are the Troops
   So dear to each heart.
T are the "Trench Feet"
   We won't let them fee...
E is the Effort
   For War Chest appeal...
R is the Rhyme
   We must write to eac...
S are the Socks,
   Which bring him such...

WISHING YOU A HAPPY XMAS
From the
Australian Comforts Funds

The Australian Comforts Fund

Writing Wallet.

Containing

Note Paper, Envelopes and Pencil.

✦ Australian medical officers at a YMCA dugout near Messines, August 1917.

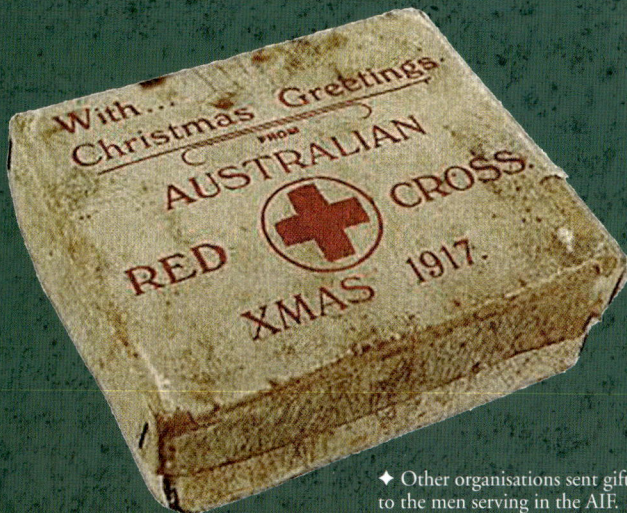

With... Christmas Greetings
AUSTRALIAN RED CROSS 1917.
XMAS

OUR FIGHTING MEN
AUSTRALIAN COMFORTS FUND

✦ Other organisations sent gifts to the men serving in the AIF.

✦ An ACF fund-raising badge.

THE GERMAN WITHDRAWAL TO THE HINDENBURG LINE — BAPAUME

For the men on both sides of the wire, the winter of 1917 was a gruelling test of endurance and morale. The Germans, still reeling from losses on the Somme and at Verdun, began a tactical withdrawal to their newly-prepared Hindenburg Line (Siegfriedstellung). This was undertaken in order to shorten the line they held and thus release a dozen infantry divisions. As they withdrew, they fought a series of rear-guard actions and carried out a scorched earth policy as they went, destroying buildings, orchards, road junctions and leaving scores of booby traps for men eager to scoop up souvenirs.

The German withdrawal along the front from south of Arras to the positions further south in the Aisne region, began late February 1917. The allied armies began cautiously probing forward across ground that had not been churned up by artillery fire. By 15 March, Australian patrols were in Beaulencourt, a few kilometres south of the town. Men of the 30th Battalion entered the ruined town of Bapaume two days later.

LAGNICOURT

The advance continued beyond Bapaume and towards the Hindenburg Line. The outpost village of Lagnicourt was captured on 26 March by units of the 7th Brigade and despite a German counter-attack, the village was held. Nearby Noreuil fell on 2 April. Three days later the Australians were along the railway embankment in front of Bullecourt. The Hindenburg Line was now less than a kilometre away. South-east of Bullecourt, the AIF captured Louverval and Doignies, with Hermies and Demicourt falling on 9 April, the opening day of the Arras Offensive. With the AIF focus now on Bullecourt (next page) and consequently suffering horrendous losses, the Germans planned a large-scale and limited objective attack against the depleted and exhausted Australians. The German attack started at 4 am on 15 April and succeeded in overrunning Lagnicourt, before pushing beyond the village and capturing Australian artillery pieces. The day was saved by the 20th and 9th Battalions who eventually pushed the Germans back, recapturing Lagnicourt. AIF losses were just over a thousand but the Germans are estimated to have lost twice this number.

✦ Captain Percy Cherry who was awarded the Victoria Cross for actions at Lagnicourt on 26 March 1917. He was killed the same day by an enemy shell and is buried at Quéant Road Cemetery, Buissy.

✦ Men of the 22nd Battalion looking for souvenirs in Bapaume. The Germans left many booby traps to catch out souvenir hunters. The Australians had done the same to the Turks when the Gallipoli Peninsula was evacuated. A timed mine exploded in the cellar of the town hall during the night of 25-26 March, killing a number of Australians as well as two visiting French politicians.

BULLECOURT 11 APRIL 1917

The huge British offensive on the Arras front began on 9 April following a lengthy period of artillery preparation that had used new flash-spotting and range-finding techniques to knock out the German artillery. Initial success was spectacular with the British divisions pushing towards Monchy le Preux and the Canadian divisions cracking the tough objective of Vimy Ridge. Bullecourt was on the southern flank of the Offensive and an integral part of the formidable Hindenburg Line defences. General Haig wanted to punch through the line here then swing north with cavalry towards the gains made by the 3rd Army. The task fell to the 4th Australian Division and the British 62nd Division.

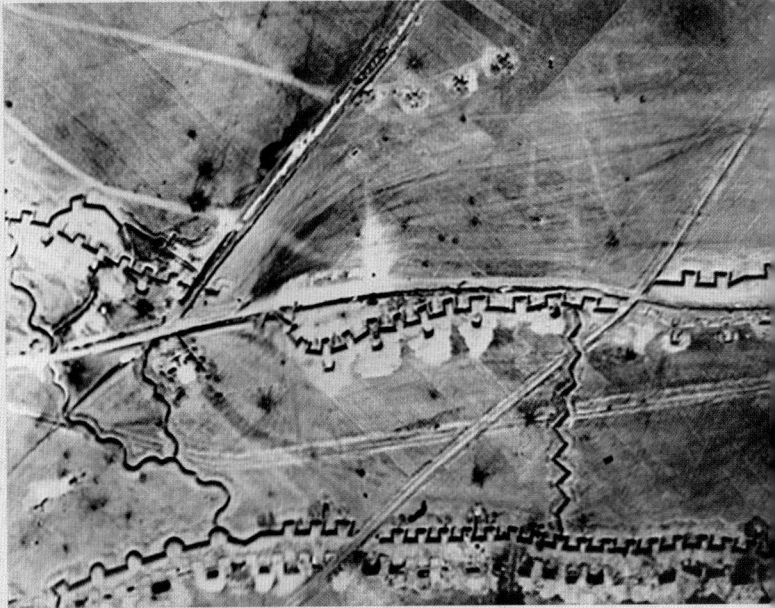

✦ Aerial view of the Hindenburg Line defences east of Bullecourt. 3 April 1917.

The Australians attacked in the early hours of 11 April from the railway embankment just south of the fortified village over snow-covered ground towards Riencourt. The belts of wire became a death trap, promised assistance from tanks failed to make any difference or indeed, in one case, caused 'friendly fire' casualties to the 46th Battalion. Despite this, some portions of the two main German trenches were captured. However, without artillery support, the men of the 4th and 12th Brigades were cut-off and subjected to attacks on their flanks.

The British attack west of the village also failed with terrible casualties. Despite the bite taken out of the Hindenburg Line, the Australians had no other alternative than to pull back. 4th Division losses were terrible; approximately 3,500 men were lost with almost 1,200 taken prisoner. Australian confidence in British command and the use of tanks was severely shaken.

✦ Anzac A relic insignia found on the Bullecourt battlefield. The A was worn on the battalion patch by men who had served at Gallipoli.

✦ Australian relic badge from the Bullecourt battlefield.

BULLECOURT — THE SECOND ATTEMPT 3 — 12 MAY 1917

With the Arras Offensive underway since 9 April, the French launched their part of the attack along the Chemin des Dames on 16 April. The attack was a disaster and led to serious unrest in the French army. The British armies now had to keep up the pressure and launch fresh attacks. On 3 May, the 1st and 3rd Armies attacked to the north, whilst on the right flank, the British 62nd and 2nd Australian Divisions faced Bullecourt once again. Unlike the first fiasco, planning for this attack was thorough. The Australians advanced behind a creeping barrage from the railway embankment at 3.45 am on 3 May, but were hit by intense machine-gun fire and the 5th Bde. attack stalled along the sunken lane in front of the embankment. The 6th Bde. succeeded in taking parts of the two German defence lines (OG1 and 2). The village itself had not been captured by the British and now posed a threat to the pocket held by the Australians in the Hindenburg Line. German attacks with flame-throwers were repulsed. By 7 May, the British 7th Division held parts of Bullecourt and the Australians pushed down OG1 trench in order to connect with the British and complete the capture of the ruined village. Further attacks along OG2 towards Bullecourt were undertaken on 12 May and the Germans at last gave up trying to recapture this part of the Hindenburg Line, withdrawing to new positions. The 1st, 2nd and 5th Divisions suffered losses of over 7,000 men.

✦ The railway embankment south of Bullecourt.

There is much to see in and around Bullecourt today. A new museum with many battlefield artefacts can be visited at Rue d'Arras. In front of the church is the 'slouch hat' Memorial to the Australians who served and fell here. Along the Rue des Australiens is the Australian Memorial Park with its digger statue, the ground here is placed between the former site of the OG1 and OG2 lines. Nearby is the Cross Memorial honouring the 2,423 Australians killed on the Bullecourt battlefields but who have no known grave. Another moving area is the railway embankment that runs south of the village. There is a signposted walking trail that incorporates this part of the battlefield.

✦ German trench map showing positions after the fighting of 1917. German lines in blue.

AUSTRALIAN TUNNELLING COMPANIES

Underground warfare and the blowing of mines under enemy trenches first appeared on the Western Front at the end of 1914. The British soon began forming specialist Royal Engineer tunnelling units mostly drawn from pre-war miners.

In Australia, two men were largely responsible for the formation of the Australian contribution to this form of warfare: Lt. J. Thomson, a mining engineer, and T.W. Edgeworth David, professor of geology at Sydney University. The mining unit was placed under the command of Lt. Col. J.A. Pollock, a mechanical engineer from Queensland. Three companies were formed and left Australia in February 1916, arriving near the front lines in France in early May of the same year. The first two companies were attached to the British 2nd Army and the third to 1st Army. Three new companies arrived in October 1916 and were absorbed by the first three.

AUSTRALIAN TUNNELLERS AT HILL 60

Hill 60 in the Ypres Salient had been the scene of much heavy fighting. Formed by the spoil from a pre-war railway cutting, it afforded good observation across the lines held by the allied troops around the battered town of Ypres. Mine warfare started there in early 1915. The Germans retook the hill in May 1915 after a gas attack and had held it since.

The 1st Australian Tunnelling Company arrived at the Hill 60 sector in early November 1916.

✦ The 1st Australian Tunnelling Company memorial at Hill 60. The mine crater is still visible, as is the Caterpillar crater the other side of the railway cutting. The damage on the memorial is the result of fighting in the vicinity in 1940.

✦ Proto mine breathing apparatus as used by tunnelling companies.

The entire area was riven with galleries, both allied and German, and great care had to be taken to avoid detection and the risk of the tunnels being blown in by camouflet counter charges. The Australian tunnellers got to work and began digging towards the German lines.

Plans had been made for a major offensive around Ypres for the second half of 1917. Before such an attack could be made, the German-held ground from Hill 60 to St.Eloi, Petit Bois, Messines and down to Ploegsteert would have to be taken. The plan was to simply blow the Germans from the face of the earth. Four days before the attack, the two mines were tamped, that is to say, the chambers where the explosives were placed sealed off to prevent the charge blowing backwards. It was now a case of waiting and hoping that the enemy did not discover the mines.

✦ A hand pump used for taking water out of tunnels and dugouts.

✦ Mine detonator.

MESSINES

The battle for Messines ridge began at 3.10 a.m. with the explosion of 19 mines (including the two of the 1st Australian Tunnelling Company at Hill 60 and Battle Wood) It has been said that the explosions were heard and even felt as far away as London. (Two of the mines failed to detonate and one blew up in a thunderstorm in 1955 !).

At the southern point of the attack sector, II Anzac Corps, comprising of the 3rd Australian Division led by Major-General John Monash and in its first action on the Western Front, the New-Zealand Division and the British 25th Division. The Germans were totally destroyed and shaken by the mines and following on the heels of a creeping artillery barrage, the Australians had taken their objectives by 5 a.m. and began digging in. This was quite a feat of arms for the 3rd Division, especially as it had suffered almost 2,000 casualties due to a German gas barrage during the approach to the jumping off positions.

Later in the day, the 4th Australian Division leapfrogged through the positions held by II Anzac and pushed forward. Fighting carried on for a further week. The vitally important high ground had been taken and held. The stage was now set for the impending large-scale offensive in the Ypres Salient.

✦ A German concrete strong-point overturned by a mine in the St.Yves sector during the opening phase of the Battle of Messines Ridge. It was at this point that the 9th Australian Infantry Brigade attacked at the southernmost point of the attack, south of the Douve River.

The surrounding area has many sites of interest. A good starting point is at Ploegsteert (known to the troops as Plugstreet) where there is a visitors centre explaining the impact of four years of war in the area. Toronto Avenue Cemetery is on the edge of the wood and contains Australian graves of men from the 3rd Australian Division, many of whom were victims of the gas attack whilst approaching the front lines. The Messines Ridge New Zealand Memorial commemorates more than 800 men of the NZ Division who died near here and who have no known grave. The Irish Peace Park stands as a memorial to Irishmen of all denominations who died during the Great War. It was near here that the 36th (Ulster) and 16th (Irish) Divisions fought during the battle for the ridge. Many of the mines, now filled with water, can be seen across the ridge.

✦ Smashed up German trenches on the Messines Ridge. It was at this point that the 9th Australien Brigade attacked at the southernmost point of the assault, south of the Douve river.

GAS EQUIPMENT

The Australians in and around Plugstreet Wood were hit hard by a German gas shell barrage during the night of 6 June. This was by no means there first brush with gas. They had been issued with anti-gas equipment upon arriving near the front lines in the spring of 1916. They had endured gas attacks on the Somme....however, it remained a much feared weapon. The following extract is by Edgar John Rule of the 14th Battalion. This unit was at St.Yves near Plugstreet Wood on 6 June 1917: "We moved at dusk, with platoons at five minute intervals. My platoon was the last.....the Hun commenced pelting gas shells right on our track....When we reached the middle of the cloud I glanced back.... One man had his small box respirator off and was struggling into his PH helmet....Several more were bolting.....We all had to go back and sort the panicky ones out. Gas is the best thing in the world to put the wind up men who have no implicit faith in their respirators, and it is only through constant training they acquire confidence."

✦ Gas alert rattle.

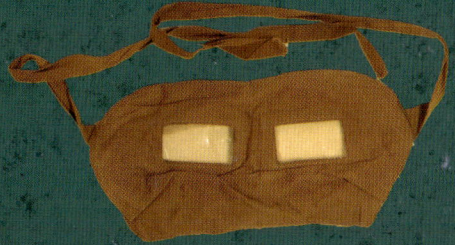

✦ Spicer anti-gas goggles, introduced in 1915.

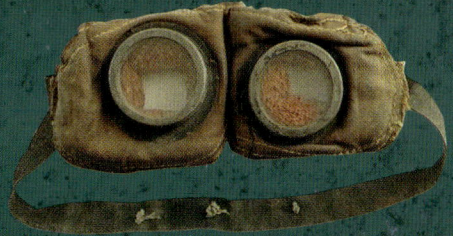

✦ Sponge anti-gas goggles.

✦ The PH anti-gas helmet was introduced at the end of 1915 and was still carried by men in 1917 as a back-up.

✦ The Small Box Respirator was introduced late 1916 and remained in service until the end of the war.

THE AIF AND THE 3RD BATTLE OF YPRES

After the successful capture of the Messines Ridge, the Commander-in-Chief, Field Marshal Haig looked towards the offensive in the Ypres Salient. The aim was to break out of the Salient, capture the vital German-held rail hub of Roulers, then advance up the Belgian coast, capturing U-Boat ports. The latter part was becoming increasingly important to Britain as the German submarine campaign was crippling the war effort and creating huge food shortages at home. Also, the French army was reeling from its huge losses in the failed Nivelle offensives and subsequent unrest (The French army took part in 3rd Ypres all the same). The onus was firmly on the British Army to carry on offensive action.

The battle was preceded by intense artillery action. Australian batteries were active in the Zillebeke area. The British attacked on 31 July and gained some early successes before the Flanders rain turned the area into a quagmire.
The Australian infantry entered into the fray on 20 September with the 1st and 2nd Divisions attacking up the Menin Road. Once again, the artillery played a vital role in softening up the enemy defences and in providing a creeping barrage behind which the men could advance. Despite being faced with staunch opposition in a landscape dotted with deadly concrete pillboxes, the Australians gained all of their objectives, but once more with a butcher's bill of 5,000 casualties.

The next phase of these bite-and-hold attacks came on 26 September, this time with the 4th and 5th Divisions. The objective was the shell-blasted Polygon Wood. The wood was taken but heavy losses were suffered south of the wood at a cluster of pillboxes near Jerk House farm. Total casualties for the two divisions were almost 5,000.

Today, the 5th Australian Division Memorial is on the Butte at Polygon Wood overlooking the large cemetery. The nearby Anzac Rest café is run by local historian Johan Vandewalle, an expert on the fighting here as well as the history of the tunnellers. The Memorial Museum, Passchendaele 1917 is a short distance away at Zonnebeke and makes for a fascinating glimpse into the period.

✦ An Australian 18-Pounder gun in action, firing on Anzac Ridge from positions near Polygon Wood. The gun has just fired and is at full recoil.

✦ 18-Pounder shell. "…. the deafening crash of the rapid firing 18–pounders, the hoarser roar of the scores of heavy guns behind them and the stupefying concussion of shrapnel and high explosive shells in the barrage in front were by now all mingled in the hideous rhythmical clamour of the perfect drum–fire barrage." Captain Alexander Ellis, 5th Division.

✦ Australian troops inspecting a captured German machine-gun near Polygon Wood.

THE SOUVENIR KING

John "Barney" Hines was born in Liverpool, England in 1873. He spent a year in the Royal Navy and also saw service in the Boer War with the King's Liverpool Regiment. He arrived in Australia in mid-1914 and volunteered for the AIF in August 1915, but ill health saw him discharged seven months later. He successfully re-enlisted in the summer and saw active service with the 45th Battalion on the Western Front from March 1917 to mid-1918 when he was once more discharged due to health reasons.

He was known for being an aggressive fighter and a hard drinker. Many of his battlefield souvenirs were later sold in order to buy alcohol.

The photograph with Hines surrounded by souvenirs was taken by famous Australian official photographer, Frank Hurley. It was published in late 1917 with the caption "Wild Eye, the souvenir king".

Post-war life was unkind to Hines and he lived in poverty until his death in 1958 in Sydney.

✦ "Barney" Hines seen here with loot taken from German prisoners after the fighting at Polygon Wood.

✦ German messtin

✦ German Feldmütze cap

✦ German steel helmet

✦ German stick grenade

BROODSEINDE RIDGE AND PASSCHENDAELE

In early October 1917, the Australians were positioned north-east of Polygon Wood and were tasked with another tough objective, Broodseinde Ridge. With the approach of winter, Haig wanted to push on and take the high ground around Passchendaele and establish his winter lines on more favourable terrain. The objective of the attack was to capture the Gheluvelt Plateau by taking the Gravenstafel Spur and Broodseinde Ridge. This would also mean that the southern flank of the line was safe from attack and also open the way for an assault on the final objective of the campaign, Passchendaele Ridge.

Four Anzac divisions attacked side-by-side on 4 October (New Zealand Division and 3rd, 2nd and 1st Australian Divisions), supported in the south by three British divisions. Advancing behind the usual creeping artillery barrage, the attack was a resounding success. All of the attacking divisions had advanced on average 1,000 yards and the 3rd Australian Division almost 2,000 yards. Success, as usual, came at a price; casualties for the Australians were 6,400. The New Zealand Division losses were over 1,800.

On 9 October, the 2nd Division, along with the British 66th Div. went onto the attack near Poelcappelle. The increasingly wet weather was turning the area into a morass and artillery fire was almost useless as many shells just plunged into the mud without exploding. The Australians were repulsed with only a further 1,200 losses to show for the day.

The Battle of Passchendaele began on 12 October, once again the 2nd Division was in action, along with the New Zealanders who suffered their blackest day of the war with hundreds of men killed by machine-gun fire whilst stuck on the wire obstacles that the artillery had been unable to destroy. Some Australians reached the ruins of Passchendaele itself but cut-off, were forced to withdraw. It would be another three weeks before the village, by now virtually erased from the cratered landscape, was finally taken.

The AIF suffered appalling losses in the campaign, between June and November, the casualty list was over 40,000. Losses for October alone ran at just under 20,000 with almost 6,500 killed in action or who died from wounds.

Tyne Cot Cemetery is nearby, one of the pillboxes captured by the Australians lies amongst the graves, crowned with the cross of sacrifice. The cemetery also has an interpretive centre. Ypres itself has the In Flanders 'Fields Museum in the rebuilt Cloth Hall. At 8 pm every evening, the buglers sound the Last Post beneath the arches of the Menin Gate. There are 6,198 AIF men commemorated here.

✦ Australian stretcher bearers on the Broodseinde Ridge, October 1917.

FEEDING THE MEN

They say that an army marches on its stomach and the Great War was no exception. Army rations, of course, were the staple diet of the men of the AIF, but they could also purchase items from civilians behind the lines or eat a meal of egg and chips in an estaminet, washed down with 'plonk or vin blanc'. Expeditionary Force Canteens were also on hand to supply a welcome change to the diet of army biscuits and bully beef. The British Army soldiers were able to receive food parcels from home but this, of course, was not an option for the Australians.

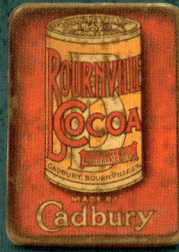

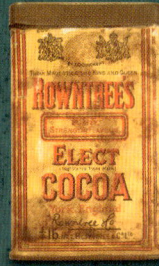

✦ Men were also able to purchase items from battalion canteens.

✦ Empty petrol tins were used to carry water to the front lines. Troops often complained of tea tasting of petrol.

✦ A group of Australian officers enjoying an improvised meal near Pozieres, 1 August 1916.

✦ Thermos food carrier.

✦ A dixie used for cooking.

✦ An Australian-made mess tin.

1918 AND THE GERMAN SPRING OFFENSIVES

The final British attack of 1917 took place at Cambrai and involved the mass use of tanks. Initial spectacular success turned to ultimate failure as German counter-attacks eventually pushed back the British troops. With the war over on the Eastern Front, the Germans were able to bring to France and Flanders many fresh divisions; they knew that they had to make one last roll of the dice before the arrival of American troops tipped the balance in favour of the Allies.

The British Army had suffered terrible losses in 1917 and now faced a manpower crisis. The Prime Minister, Lloyd-George, did not want to send more troops to be used in what he considered wasteful campaigns and precious British divisions had also been sent to Italy to shore up the front after the Caporetto disaster. Added to this was the French insistence that the British take over more of the front line south of the river Somme. The scene was set for a military disaster.

The German hammer blow fell on 21st March. At 4.40 am, they began the heaviest artillery bombardment thus seen in the war with over a million shells fired in five hours. Despite stiff resistance, often to the last man, the British 5th Army divisions began to give way and two days later were in retreat across the old Somme battlefields, sacred ground that had been paid for with the blood of thousands of men back in 1916. By 26 March, the Germans were poised to take the symbolic town of Albert. It was on this same day that the Allies held a conference at Doullens and decided to make French Maréchal Foch the head of allied armies. During the same evening, the Germans entered Albert and a front line was formed along the high ground just beyond the shattered town.

✦ A German photograph showing British dead in one of the redoubts captured on 21 March 1918.

DERNANCOURT

In the winter of 1917-18, the AIF was in the front lines between Ypres and Armentères. With the dreadful news of the retreat further south, the Australians received orders to prepare to move. Men of the 4th Division and New Zealanders were in the new front line near Hébuterne by the evening of 26 March. Monash's 3rd Division arrived at Doullens and were transported towards Albert, by now in German hands. By the 28th, Australian units were now present in the front lines at Villers-Bretonneux, Dernancourt, Morlancourt and Hébuterne.

The village of Morlancourt is situated roughly two and half miles south-west of Albert. Just to the north of the village is a railway embankment that was the scene of very bitter fighting on 28 March. The men of the 47th and 48th Battalions were spread out thinly when the Germans attacked from Albert and along the river Ancre. With the help of a British battalion, they repulsed no less than nine attacks from a vastly superior enemy force. The thinly-manned outposts along the embankment were penetrated but the enemy was thrown back. Two days later the Germans attacked again from Albert, this time without artillery preparation. The men of the 11th Brigade fought off three attacks, leaving the ground in front of them littered with German dead.

The Germans attacked again in strength on 5 April all along the front. The Australians had put the intervening time to good use and had dug support lines along the high ground behind the railway embankment lines. The German intention was to reach the road at the top of the slope then swing their advance towards the vital rail hub of Amiens. Once more it was the 47th and 48th Battalions that bore the brunt of the assault. Flares were fired into the sky to call down a support barrage but due to heavy mist these were not seen. The third enemy attack broke through the embankment and forced the Australians back to the support lines around where the military cemetery now stands today. A counter-attack in the early evening pushed the enemy back to the first support line on the slope. The day was saved, but once again casualties were heavy with 4th Division losses reaching 1,100.

✦ Parachute flare crate and relic Webley flare gun found near Dernancourt.

✦ Webley flare gun. Flares, or Very Lights, were used in daytime as well as at night. Different coloured flares could be used to call down artillery fire on German counter-attacks. The flares fired at Dernancourt to call down artillery fire along the S.O.S. line were not seen due to heavy mist.

✦ A packet of flare cartridges.

VILLERS-BRETONNEUX

"Fini retreat, Madame, beaucoup Australiens ici"

4 APRIL

The Germans felt that another concerted push would take them to Amiens. If this city fell, a vital rail hub would be lost and perhaps force the British and Empire forces out of the war.

Early in the morning of 4 April, the Germans advanced on either side of the arrow-straight main road towards Amiens. British units were forced back or gave up their positions, leaving Australian units with their flanks unprotected and, therefore, obliged to withdraw. Another German attack in the afternoon almost succeeded in capturing Villers-Bretonneux but a counter-attack by the 36th Battalion and a British unit forced the enemy to withdraw.

✦ German A7V tank 'Mephisto' was in action at Villers-Bretonneux on 24 April. It was recovered by the Australians and eventually shipped back home and displayed at the Queensland Museum.

24 – 26 APRIL

A new large-scale attack was launched on the town in the early morning, supported by thirteen huge German A7V tanks. The world's first tank-on-tank engagement took place that day south of the town. A few hours later, the enemy had pushed the British defenders back and captured the town as well as some ground beyond it. Two Australian infantry brigades were brought forward to recapture the town. A night counter-attack was planned. The 15th Brigade, 5th Division would sweep around the area north of the town whilst the 14th Bde. near Vaire Wood would push forward. To the south, the 13th Brigade, 4th Division, would attack near Cachy. The Australians swept forward under the cover of nightfall and pushed the enemy back in hand-to-hand fighting. The Germans pulled back under the threat of encirclement, leaving many men behind in the town. Villers-Bretonneux was now firmly back in allied hands and the Germans had been taught a harsh lesson.

What to see. Villers-Bretonneux is home to the Australian National Monument on Hill 104 on the road to Corbie. It was inaugurated in 1938 and bears the names of 10,770 Australians who died on the Western Front and who have no known grave. A new John Monash visitor's centre is due to open here in 2018. The town itself has a Franco-Australian Museum in the school building which was funded by school children from the state of Victoria after the war. A kilometre along the D168 to Cachy is a small monument commemorating the first ever tank-versus-tank battle of 24 April 1918.

✦ "Don't forget Australia." French children tend Australian graves near Villers-Bretonneux in 1919. The town retains strong links to this day with Australia.

✦ The first tank-versus-tank battle memorial near Cachy.

Ici, le 24 Avril 1918, eut lieu le premier combat mondial entre tanks allemands et britanniques.

Here, on the 24th of April 1918, the first ever tank battle took place between German and British armor.

Hier, am 24. April 1918, findet der erste Weltangriff zwischen deutschen und britishen Panzerwagen.

PERSONAL ITEMS

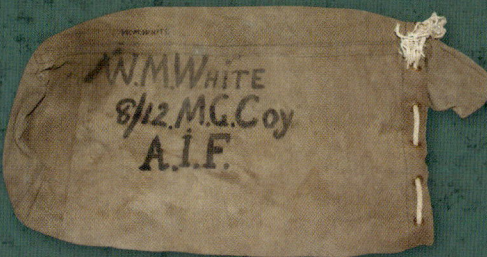

✦ Kit bag belonging to W.M. White of 8/15 Machine Gun Company, AIF.

✦ Cigarette case with the AIF insignia.

✦ AIF insignia.

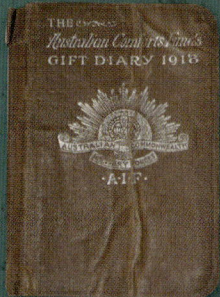

✦ Australian Comforts Fund diary.

✦ Australian Imperial Force paybook.

✦ Australian-made field dressing.

✦ Various identity tags.

✦ "Trench art" identity tag.

✦ Soldier's 'housewife' roll and personal hygiene items.

✦ Australian soldier's messtin.

THE DEMISE OF THE RED BARON 21 APRIL 1918

Freiherr Manfred Von Richthofen, better known as the Red Baron, is no doubt the most famous of all World War One pilots. He was credited with 80 kills.

By late March, the German advance allowed his squadron to be based at Cappy on the Somme river. Late morning on 21 April 1918, he was chasing a rookie Canadian pilot and closing in for his 81st kill. Another Canadian pilot, Captain Arthur 'Roy' Brown, swooped down and opened fire on Richthofen's red Fokker triplane, forcing the German ace to take evasive action. The Red Baron then focused on chasing the camel aircraft that he had originally been targeting. Flying low over the Australian-held Morlancourt ridge, he came under ground fire. Hit in the chest, he had just enough life left in him to bring his plane down.

'Roy' Brown was credited with the kill. Today, however, it is largely accepted that this would not have been the case given the angle of the entry and exit wound later observed on the Red Baron's body. More recent research has established that he was indeed the victim of ground fire. Sgt. Cedric Popkin of the Australian 24th Machine-Gun Company fired twice, once as the German pilot approached frontally and again from the side. Other researchers have identified another two men who fired at the plane. Both were Lewis gunners serving with the 53rd Battery,

✦ The crash site today on the Morlancourt ridge near Corbie. The 3rd Australian Division Memorial stands a short drive away along the D1 road above the village of Sailly-Laurette.

14th Field Artillery Brigade, Royal Australian Artillery; their names are W.J. Evans and R. Buie.

The Red Baron was buried at Bertangles, north of Amiens, with full military honours by members of N°3 Squadron, Australian Flying Corps. His body was moved to Fricourt German cemetery after the war, then finally back to Germany.

✦ Men of N°3 Squadron, AFC, examine remains of Richthofen's plane. The wrecked aircraft was picked clean by souvenir hunting AIF men on Morlancourt ridge.

THE 1ST DIVISION AIF
AND THE SECOND GERMAN OFFENSIVE

Due to the famous AIF actions stemming the German tide on the Somme, those of the 1st Australian Division, further north, tend to be overlooked. The Division, however, played a vital role in halting the second of the German offensives that began on 9 April 1918 in the Armentières sector.

Using similar tactics to those of 21 March, the German 6th army swept forward against the Portuguese Division and some British divisions that had been placed in this quiet sector after being severely mauled on the Somme. The weakened line soon gave way; Armentières was abandoned and the Germans were soon at Bailleul, a town which fell shortly after. With the left flank of the line in the air, the agonizing, but tactically sound decision was made to pull back from ground in the Ypres Salient further north; terrain that had cost so much blood six months earlier.

✦ A German trench mortar captured during a raid in June 1916 on Mont de Merris, south-west of Bailleul.

The 1st Division did not even have time to detrain as its units arrived in the Somme sector. They were sent back north and arrived at the vital rail hub of Hazebrouck on 12 April. The Australians were effectively the only combat capable troops between the Germans and the channel ports, the loss of which would have dealt a mortal blow to the BEF. The next day saw the four of the Division's battalions holding a vast section of front line almost ten kilometres in length. Contact with the enemy came a day later at Vieux-Berquin and the high ground at Merris to the north. Fresh British and French troops also helped to bring the German advance on Hazebrouck to an end and the focus of the offensive moved north towards the looming mass of Mont Kemmel.

The 1st Division remained in the Bailleul sector until late July and the intervening period was marked by frequent Australian raids against the German front line and outposts. The 1st Division men soon gained morale ascendancy over the enemy.

✦ Livens gas projector base from the Merris sector. These were buried in the ground in batteries with just the muzzles protruding and were electronically activated.

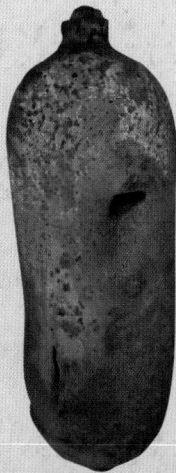

✦ The Livens projectors fired gas canisters up to a range of just under a mile.

✦ British Newton trench mortar projectile.

LE HAMEL

The Battle of Le Hamel, 4 July 1918, stands out as a masterpiece of a well-planned attack with limited objectives. The planning, carried out by Lt. Gen. John Monash, brought into play all of the tactical innovations that had been learnt at such a high cost throughout the war. Medical supplies and small arms ammunition would be dropped by parachute during the advance and tanks used to bring up further supplies instead of using the follow-up waves of infantry.

Units involved were brigades from the 2nd, 3rd, and 4th Divisions, with the latter providing the bulk of the attacking force and the 6th Division involved in a feint attack near Buire-sur-Ancre. The battle also stands out as one where American forces were under foreign command for the first time. Indeed, it was deemed that the American soldiers could gain precious battle experience. Men of the US 33rd Division were allocated to the attack. The initial ten companies were reduced to four when General Pershing heard of the plans to use US troops.

The attack was launched at 03:10 hrs on 4th July with a creeping barrage provided by over 600 guns. The fiercest fighting took place at Pear Trench, the village of Le Hamel and Vaire and Hamel Woods. Monash had planned for a ninety minute attack and the objectives were indeed taken with only three minutes added to this estimated time frame. The Germans, as ever, pre-

✦ The Australian Corps Memorial Park at Le Hamel.

pared a counter-attack which was duly delivered on 5 July. Despite some modest gains, they were eventually driven back by the Australians.

Success came at a price; allied casualties were approximately 1,400 with the already depleted Australians losing over 1,000 men, including 800 dead. However, the Germans had suffered heavy losses too, an estimated 2,000 killed and over 1,500 taken prisoner and they had lost the advantage of the high ground around Le Hamel.

Today, the Australian Corps Memorial stands above the village. Remains of trench lines can be seen and an observation table and information panels give an excellent description of events that took place there.

✦ Australian and American troops on the Le Hamel battlefield.

THE AMIENS OFFENSIVE

By August 1918, the Germans had exhausted their final reserves of men and military strength in a series of huge offensives. The French had been the first to successfully hit back on 18 July in the Villers-Cotterêts region. The region chosen for the next counter offensive was Amiens. The attack would involve French, British, Canadian and Australian forces, as well as some elements of the US 33rd Division.

Once again using tactics that had proven successful at Le Hamel, the attacking troops advanced on 8 August behind a curtain of artillery fire provided by 2,000 guns, with tanks and aircraft providing support. The French, without tank support, attacked forty-five minutes later on the southern flank of the attack.

The surprise attack was a staggering success, the deepest point of penetration being 13 kilometres from the start point. German losses ran at an estimated 30,000 and Ludendorff later stated that it was the black day of the German army; not so much due to the ground lost, but more due to the obvious decline in morale.

The Amiens offensive heralded an end to prolonged trench warfare and saw a return to a war of movement that would end a hundred days later.

✦ Sir John Monash GGMG, KCB, VD. 1865-1931. Born in Melbourne to Jewish-Prussian parents, Monash became the first Australian to lead the AIF. He was the architect of victories at Le Hamel and Amiens and is sometimes referred to as the father of the blitzkrieg for his methodical set-piece attacks combining all-arms cooperation. He was knighted by the King four days after the start of the Amiens offensive.

PÉRONNE
MONT ST QUENTIN

The incredible allied thrust had taken the Allies as far as 19 kilometres. The French commander, Foch, now supreme allied commander, wanted the advance to continue. Field Marshal Haig, however, refused, preferring a fresh attack by the 3rd Army in the Albert region. This latest offensive was launched on 21 August and within a week had pushed the Germans back across the old battlefields of 1916.

The Australians found themselves faced with the obstacle of the town of Péronne and the fortified high ground of Mont St. Quentin that commanded the battered town and the surrounding area. The Somme was crossed on 30 August. The plan of attack was once more conceived by Monash and his staff. It was decided to attack the hill frontally across marshy ground, however, the latter proved to be an impassable obstacle to the men of the 2nd Division. The hill was attacked the next day and captured. A German counter-attack pushed the Australians back off the crest of the hill but a fresh attack the next day finally captured this vital high ground. This was the last defendable ground for the Germans who now had no other choice but to pull back to the Hindenburg Line from where they had started back in March. Péronne fell to the men of the 5th Division.

✦ Péronne does not forget its Australian liberators.

✦ Australian dead in the wire defences near Anvil Wood just south of Mont St Quentin.
Success was, once more, achieved at high cost; the already dangerously depleted Australian units lost a further 3,000 casualties.

✦ The original 2nd Division AIF Memorial was inaugurated in the presence of Maréchal Foch in 1925. The sculpture, by Australian artist Charles Web Gilbert, portrays a digger on the point of running his bayonet through a German imperial eagle. Deemed offensive by the occupying Germans in the Second World War, it was removed and subsequently destroyed. It was replaced in 1971 by a proud digger. The nearby Péronne museum of the Great War has, with the help of the Australian government, recently opened a history trail on Mont St Quentin where original trench lines can still be seen.

BREAKING THE HINDENBURG LINE AND THE FINAL BATTLES

The victorious drive that had started for the Australians on 8 August had left the AIF with a manpower crisis. The volunteer system had shown its limitations and compounded to this, Prime Minister Hughes insisted that men who had been out since the beginning should be allowed six months leave back home; further depleting battalions that desperately needed men. This was somewhat allayed, however, when Monash was given operational command of two American divisions, the 27th and 30th.

The next obstacle was the crossing of the Hindenburg Line to which the Germans had withdrawn once more as they had in March 1917. The Australians had sinister memories of this defensive line where they had suffered grievous losses in 1917 in two attacks at Bullecourt. The sector of the defences facing the Australians was integrated into a deeply positioned canal of which a portion ran along a deep shell-proof tunnel, and which was riddled with concrete bunkers and machine-gun emplacements.

The fight for the Hindenburg Line began along the former British lines that the Germans had turned into outpost defences. The 1st and 4th Divisions AIF, with British units on each flank, attacked on 18 September and successfully carried their objectives. The main attack went in on 29 September, the US Divisions attacked first and the Australians then leapfrogged through but, due to the inexperience of the courageous Americans and their failure to mop up points of resistance, the Australians were soon in trouble. Determined fighting pushed the Germans back to their last defensive line by 3 October. Although the men did not realise it at the time, they would soon be facing their final battle. The last obstacle facing the Australians of the 2nd Division was the village of Montbrehain which sat upon a hill beyond the last of the Hindenburg Line's defences. The village was taken on 5 October after house-to-house fighting. The exhausted men of the AIF, who had suffered 27,000 casualties since 8 August, were then withdrawn and would see no further fighting. They had done their bit.

✦ Calvaire Cemetery, Montbrehain where some of the last AIF men to be killed in action are buried.

✦ The 4th Division Memorial near Bellenglise where the Division fought its final action in capturing part of the Hindenburg Line outpost defences, losing more than a thousand casualties. It is the most eastern of the AIF divisional memorials.

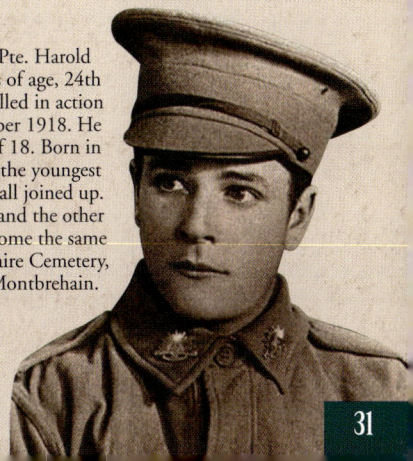

✦ One of the last to fall. Pte. Harold Federal Hardy, 22 years of age, 24th Infantry Battalion, AIF. Killed in action at Montbrehain 5 October 1918. He enlisted in 1915 at the age of 18. Born in Brunswick, Victoria, he was the youngest of three brothers who all joined up. One was killed in 1917 and the other wounded and returned home the same year. Harold lies in Calvaire Cemetery, Montbrehain.

✦ The steep banks of the St Quentin Canal that formed part of the Hindenburg Line defences.

AUSTRALIAN VICTORIA CROSS WINNERS – WESTERN FRONT 1916 – 1918

The Victoria Cross is the British Army's greatest decoration for valour in the presence of the enemy. 628 were awarded during World War One. Australian soldiers won 64 Victoria Crosses in the various theatres in which they saw action (Gallipoli, Palestine). The following list is of those won on the Western Front.

Pte. J.W.A. Jackson – Bois Grenier – 25-26 June 1916
Pte. J. Leak - Pozières – 23 July 1916
Lt. A.S. Blackburn - Pozières – 23 July 1916
Pte. T. Cooke - Pozières – 24-25 July 1916
Sgt. Castleton - Pozières – 28 July 1916
Pte. M. O'Meara – Pozières – 9 – 12 August 1916
Capt. H.W. Murray - Stormy Trench, Somme – 4-5 February 1917
Capt. P.H. Cherry – Lagnicourt – 26 March 1917
Pte. J.C. Jenson – Noreuil – 2 April 1917
Capt. J.E. Newland – Boursies – Lagnicourt – 8-15 April 1917
Pte. T.J.B. Kenny - Hermies – 9 April 1917
Sgt. J.W. Whittle – Boursies – 8 – 15 April 1917
Lt. C. Pope – Louverval – 15 April 1917
Cpl. G.J. Howell – Bullecourt – 6 May 1917
Lt. R.V. Moon – Bullecourt – 12 May 1917
Capt. R.C. Grieve – Messines – 7 June 1917
Pte. J. Carroll – Messines – 7 – 11 June 1917
2nd Lt. F. Birks – Glencourse Wood – 20 September 1917
Pte. R.R. Inwood – Polygon Wood – 20 – 21 September 1917
Sgt. J.J. Dwyer – Zonnebeke – 26 September 1917
Cpl. P.J. Bugden – Polygon Wood – 26 – 28 September 1917
L/Cpl. W. Peeler – Broodseinde – 4 October 1917
Sgt. L. McGee – Broodseinde – 4 October 1917
Capt. C.S. Jeffries – Passchendaele – 12 October 1917
Sgt. S.R. McDougall – Dernancourt – 28 March 1918
Lt. P.V. Storkey – Hangard Wood (Villers-Bretonneux) – 7 April 1918

Lt. C.W.K. Sadlier – Villers-Bretonneux – 24 – 25 April 1918
Sgt. W. Ruthven – Ville-sur-Ancre – 19 May 1918
Cpl. P. Davey – Merris – 28 June 1918
L/Cpl. T.L. Axford – Le Hamel – 4 July 1918
Pte. H. Dalziel – Le Hamel – 4 July 1918
Cpl. W. Brown – Villers-Bretonneux – 6 July 1918
Lt. A.C. Borella – Villers -Bretonneux – 17-18 July 1918
Lt. A.E. Gaby – Villers Bretonneux – 8 August 1918
Pte. R.M. Beatham – Rosières – 9 August 1918
Sgt. P.C. Statton – Proyart – 12 August 1918
Lt. W.D. Joynt – Herleville Wood – 23 August 1918
Lt. L.D. McCarthy – Madame Wood – 23 August 1918
L/Cpl. B.S. Gordon – Bray – 26 – 27 August 1918
Pte. G. Cartwright – Péronne – 31 August 1918
Pte. W.M. Currey – Péronne – 1 September 1918
Sgt. A.D. Lowerson – Mont St. Quentin – 1 September 1918
Pte. R. Mactier - Mont St. Quentin – 1 September 1918
Lt. E.T. Towner - Mont St. Quentin – 1 September 1918
Cpl. A.H. Buckley – Péronne – 1 September 1918
Cpl. A.C. Hall – Péronne – 1 – 2 September 1918
Cpl. L.C. Weathers – Péronne – 2 September 1918
Sgt. M.V. Buckley – Le Verguier – 18 September 1918
Pte. J.P. Woods – Le Verguier – 18 September 1918
Mjr. B.A. Wark – Bellicourt – 29 September – 1 October 1918
Pte. J. Ryan – Bellicourt – 30 September 1918
Lt. J. Maxwell – Estrées – 3 October 1918
Lt. G.M. Ingram – Montbrehain – 5 October 1918

GOING HOME

The fighting for the infantry was over at Montbrehain, but some artillery units and the Australian Flying Corps continued until the end of war. When the Armistice came, two of the AIF divisions remained in the Le Cateau area and the three others on the Channel coast at Abbeville. Four of the divisions were in Belgium around Charleroi in April 1919 as the wheels of returning home were slowly set in motion. A system of first over first to return was installed and the proud AIF slowly faded away from France and Flanders.

Losses for such a small nation were terrible, from a 1914 population of 4.9 million, 416,809 men had voluntarily enlisted, some 38.7% of the male population aged between 18 and 44.

Australians killed in action (in all theatres) totalled 60,284. A further 155,133 were wounded and 4,044 taken prisoner. Now was the time to remember and construct memorials for those who would never see home, memorials that still stand proudly today on the rolling Picardy countryside or the former battlefields of the Ypres salient.

✦ A British pattern mess tin found near the site of the Villers-Bretonneux memorial during work extending the car-park.

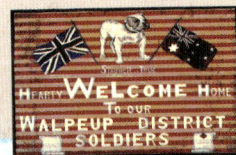

✦ Victoria School in Villers-Bretonneux. Built in 1924-27, the school was a gift from the school children of the state of Victoria.